MYSTERIES OF THE HORIZON

MYSTERIES OF

THE HORIZON

LAWRENCE RAAB

1972
DOUBLEDAY & COMPANY, INC.
GARDEN CITY, NEW YORK

For my friends

8 | |
R

Some of these poems first appeared in the following publications: *The New Orleans Review*, "The Shadow on the Wall"; *The American Scholar*, "Voices Answering Back: The Vampires," "Hero on His Way Home," "Magritte: The Song of the Glass Keys and the Cape of Storms"; *Poetry*, "Sunday," "Walking Alone," Copyright © 1969 by Modern Poetry Association, and *Poetry*, "Eight Landscapes from the Tarot Deck," Copyright © 1971 by Modern Poetry Association; *The Magazine of Fantasy and Science Fiction*, "Vampires," Copyright © 1970 by Mercury Press, Inc.; *Shenandoah*, "To Lorca"; *Poetry Northwest*, "The Asylum Years," Copyright © 1971 by Poetry Northwest; *Arion*, "Spleen," Copyright © 1969 by Arion; *Southern Poetry Review*, "The Summer Vacation"; *The Antioch Review*, "At Evening: One Way and Then Another," Copyright © 1972 by The Antioch Press; *The New York Quarterly Review*; "The Survivors," Copyright © 1972 by The New York Quarterly Poetry Review; *The Atlantic Monthly*, "The Dream of Rousseau," Copyright © 1972 by The Atlantic Monthly Company; *Encounter*, "Figure with Hypodermic Syringe"; *Voyages*, "Ice," Copyright © 1972 by Voyages, Inc., solely owned by William F. Claire.

Grateful acknowledgment is made to the following publishers: Farrar, Straus & Giroux, Inc., for five lines from the poem "Seven Charms for a New Day" from the book *In the Trail of the Wind* edited by John Bierhorst; New Directions Publishing Corporation for eleven lines, passim, from "Somnabule Ballad," translated by Stephen Spender and J. L. Gili from *The Selected Poems of Federico Garcia Lorca*, edited by Francisco Garcia Lorca and Donald M. Allen. Copyright 1955 by New Directions Publishing Corporation. Reprinted by permission of New Directions Publishing Corporation; Alfred A. Knopf, Inc., for excerpt from the poem "Arrival at the Waldorf," Copyright 1942 by Wallace Stevens, from *The Collected Poems of Wallace Stevens*.

CONTENTS

1

THE SHADOW ON THE WALL

At the beginning of my hour the wind
falls. In the thick branch of my dark
the sun howls. When only light
carries the river along, you see me.
Turn three times around, close
the left eye only, and I grow.

In tricks of light I come to live.
Beneath the dark my own dark slides.
I divide upon stones.
I become too many to see.

From what day leaves behind
I have made signs: Beware the Deep Woods.
Do Not Think You Are Ever Alone.
All directions I give where I stand.
Tree branch reaches out. I am the tree.

And I am the first dream you find,
now on the hill the color
of wind, now on the shore
the color of bones,
and of rain, saying:

I can be anyone you need.

AN OLD PHOTOGRAPH FROM VERMONT

We are too far away to see the pattern
of the embroidery she holds against
the back of the chair in front of the house
with its open windows and two screened doors.

Nor is her face clear, though she seems
to smile. Curves of a mountain blur off
to each side, and a pair of apple trees
press thin shade upon the walls.

It is late summer, blackberry season.

Beyond fields which we cannot see, a stream
burrows into the cool side of a hill. Further,
in wild country where she has never gone,
one dark pond reflects a circle of spruce,

and the birds are silent, for this is the time
just before a storm, when leaves grow heavy,
and your heart thickens for no reason.

Why, then, is she smiling,

as the first gust falls into the yard, as husband
or father calls from the house, telling her
to come in, far off telling her that, as

she strays into the crush of weeds, at the edge
of the field, beyond garden, barn, and all
of us. You would think she believes

the wind will carry her away.

THE HERO ON HIS WAY HOME

A gathering of whiteness before morning
Rough sheets tightened against the wind
Always it is the same kind of beginning
Gifts and wishes   ceremonies of farewell
Slowly the ship leans toward another island
where they will not know your face
though long ago you stopped growing old

Tonight while Orion floats above the mast
and all directions for once seem clear
you dream of losing hold
reckless between the fingers of a god
whose name you can never remember
And you think If only I could begin correctly
I might discover which way to turn

Everything must be lost
wealth   arms   all companions
Your ship groans beneath you
Gray water rattles into the wood
Speak to the dead and what do they say
I died for you please bury me
What can I say to help tell me what can I say

You will remember
the stuck whine of their tongues   years later
in the scrubbed hall
under the sane roof
while your son grows restless by the fire
your wife more cautious and removed

You will feel a hand tremble upon a knee
as if something had always been wrong
and turning you will whisper
to whatever goddess favors that hour
Lady, listen

Gently then she tells you
where it was you were never going

AN HISTORICAL MEMORY

The wind jumped
in the valley
where the miners were returning

In the dark the river moved beside them
Thin shadows melted from the curtains
and the cold found its way everywhere

into the school which was locked
into the stores which were closed
into the church where candles

folded against themselves like flowers
Abandoned to a different season
the hero draws his escapes together

from a country bordered by seas
blue as the center of a flame
like a mirror of the way he had come

and where he might choose to be
emptied of these departures
The moon breaks through

The wind comes out of the mountains
as the ends of another year
tie themselves together

On their way home
the breaths of the miners rise
like small clouds emptied of words

The wind touches them
and divides

AFTER COLONUS

When you have found the place to wait
something begins to be remembered
What you thought lost has followed you
disguised as a friend
A flight of sparrows passes over trees
calling a name you almost know
Pale squares of fields blur
into a confusion of roadways

They will all lead into
one old and unbelievable courtyard
crowded with messengers weeping
through their heavy stories
If those garbled histories are not yours
if the seer's birds break into smoke
and pastured stones do not cry out

May any prayer be offered
How then will the body wear
its suspected shame
Though messengers grow tired and leave
though no oracle will speak
nevertheless
it is not possible to turn away

What man has not felt
a gray shadow coast across his dreams
and night after night tracked back
to find the place
where three roads meet

Having no city's grief to tend
you stand there
more alone than any king
wondering which roads
turn toward disaster
and which toward home

THE SURVIVORS

Somehow they continue
to find the way here

with their ruined hands
and the bandages over their eyes

with their voices tied up
trailing behind like baggage

they continue to find
the roads that are left

though after they pass
the roads are taken away

and arrival is moved
another day ahead

COMMON GROUND

There are   blue flowers in a jar on my table

It is   raining here and in other cities

This is not   a comfortable place to wait

Each could be made a beginning   as
this one begins   three times
though no more worthy of your trust
by confessing to the problem

laying an unsatisfactory trail of words
across the page as if to meet you
half way

or at the point of a proper opening   glorious
with what might touch you
and lead us both to life   from one
place to another   into a memory

of years ago or of last night
as simple as a sentence   as clear
as the space around a name

He hid the body in a cave

The Countess turned away from the window

After her death he could not bear to live by the sea

THE RULES, THE STORY,
AND THE WAY OUT

The forests are crowded with deceptions,
perfect fruit glazed with a subtle poison.
Beware also of mirrors and masks.
But if the shoe fits, wear it.

If the sorcerer invites you to his
cottage in the country, remember
revelations are dangerous to ignore.
But if the coach comes apart, hang on.

You will discover the princess
by her good looks, and the prince likewise.
But if love cannot quicken their dreams,
you know where to turn.

You know, by now, the staleness of salt,
and the old tune of your heart enough to know
that it has not broken because
this story failed to include you.

THE SUMMER VACATION

The clear sun falls on the floor
in the shape of a window

She waves at me

A house rushes by
Someone to the side is speaking

The house restores itself and is gone

Father grins
He gathers the family toward him

An ocean blurs into the weather of that day
streaked with what followed it here

The baby peeks through her wrinkled fingers
Father leans toward the wheel of his car
Mother looks up and is
not quite sure of what to do

her beautiful face loosening into the light
that surrounds her

and fastens them all to the shelter of this room
where I

am keeping them alive

FOR THE ANIMALS

for my mother

I call to them
with the names you gave me

waiting for the new moon
watching for the trembling in the trees
where the wind hides out at night

I call their secret names and they
come to me   finding
the home we made for them
so much like our own   with yellow flowers
and books   clear windows   a door at each end
to go out and come back in
chairs and a good table and everything
you could want

Your poem fills with animals

Woodchuck and beaver   the sly fox
the pompous rabbit   otter   deer
raccoon   and owl

In my house there are more of us
than I ever thought we knew
smiling and bringing presents for you

The perfect wings of the owl lift with the wind
The earth hugs the mole as a friend
The bear offers honey from his hands

I let myself fall
into the soft arms of animals and then
into their dreams

all of our secrets
returning to me   falling back to me
carrying me home

AT EVENING: ONE WAY AND THEN
ANOTHER

The tree leaves itself behind

leaning toward this window
to lend what it can

The wind loses direction
while hoops and swings unravel into their darkness

while my hands are
again begging the same questions
asking for change
asking where it
all was spent

I have given up answering

I make my way from room to room
crouching at the cold locks with a ring of keys
waiting to be caught

But I save what I can
I piece together whatever I find
in the bottoms of envelopes and drawers
in the broken ends of things
when their reasons have failed

I lay one against another

So the wind comes out of the mountains
and drifts through the bells of the town

So the river travels under two stone bridges
going and coming like a friend

And broken magazines from the war

when the stitching loosens
their bent faces turn back
to what they were without me

Part of this too
is missing

the same part

Into the shape of its absence

names are passed like coins to beggars

Later the dream of strangers repeats itself
a shelf of calm before morning

when the dead open those hands
and you promise them everything because
what is there to lose

while the ends of the rain upon the roof
make a small thin sound

and beyond the window a maze of broken
threads fall
into the long grass   into the fields
into another place
like this one

and as far away

SEVEN CHARMS FOR A NEW DAY

It was the wind that gave them life. It is the wind
that comes out of our mouths now that gives us life.
When this ceases to blow we die. In the skin at the
tips of our fingers we see the trail of the wind; it
shows us where the wind blew when our ancestors
were created.

—Navajo poem

1

Everywhere I discover the signs of ancestors

footprints lightly
lightly bending
this way
in new grass

2

Blue air opens around me
wind brushes my eyes   and wind again
enters the circles of my fingers

3

Inside the seed of the wind
children are born

Such a small place
but a heart can be lost in it

4

A tree rises from a familiar path
a white tree blossoming in a thorny road

What was lost has been here

and remains
kept close
in the rising of the light
in this sudden light rising
from the belly of a long and difficult night

5

Sleeping water stirs in the hollow of a rock
My face enters it my hands
tremble in it

Everything hides within itself
water inside water
flower inside flower

the bright seed inside the seed

6

I invent new signs in the fresh earth

The voices of birds will comfort me
The roots of unnamed plants will cure me
An amulet of stone will protect me
if I believe in it

7

And if I find you
at the end of the long falling of the wind

I will bend down
to touch your face

I will add my breath
like this
to yours

LIKE THIS

Choose a stone and turn it over
Lean through the flowering shrubs
and discover a path

This is the way to begin

Let the stream fall into its old place
and watch beneath the current
for the markings
taking their shape

Don't speak too quickly
All of this
lives on inside your life
There is no hurry

Don't explain the meaning
of what your hands may chance to find
They have their own dreams
Trust them

As for me
I go on
learning where to stand
counting up the names
polishing the charms
for my pockets

I can walk out into the wind any time
into a sudden change of season
Then I turn around looking back

It is four years ago
and I am stepping from a ship

at night in a new country

2

VAMPIRES

So tender to the light it breaks them—
sunset rising, midnight's their noon,
earth's ancients following cock's call
home to sleep. They cannot take death
too seriously, who half-live each
borrowed day, alone in a shuttered room,
slender of face and eyes sensibly shut,
though stake and cross shake their dreams.
Sir and Lady, hide quickly your pale daughters
at dark's drawing on. These shapes
frequent old mansions where no mirror
may touch that softest step,
nor will dust or cobweb break as they glide
upon a play of dreams, and prey towards blood.
At one touch all hungers turn simple,
indifferent to dying. Linked to wolf's cry,
small as a bat upon the night wind,
still they fear the forms good men
bear against them, so do not ask
for pity ever. Yet if mischance
find their eyes seared in a blaze of first sun,
or if villages of arms all waving Christ
drive one back upon his coffin's lid,
go easy with your stake, sir.
Pain sits on their hearts, heavy as ours.

NOISE

The ice cream is melting
because the refrigerator has stopped

Of course the faucet leaks

And on toward three in the morning
the pointed footsteps continue upstairs
then voices and another blur of music

Outside a truck bulls its way through the rain
shifting down to make the long hill

I bask in violence until my hands shake

No one will be safe from me
scrawling threats inside the elevator
obscenities on the tenants' doors
concealing small bombs among the garbage
and bursting at last into the lobby
with plastic vines waving from each huge hand
I smash mirrors and windows
pull free calendars and paintings
jam the doors and take no prisoners   so finally

I arm myself

with a clear eye and a hair trigger
with a single needle of light cutting through the evening
down onto the windshield of the truck
onto the forehead of the driver who squints
stupidly into the rain   one hand
on the wheel one foot on the clutch

I cradle
the heavy barrel in my left palm
and lean forward to meet him

THIS EXAMINATION WILL NOT COUNT
TOWARD YOUR FINAL GRADE

Suddenly a stranger rushes forward

Who are you to speak he says

I pay my rent
I have canceled checks for proof
I always place my bets
on the even numbers
You tell me

I never said I knew
what I was looking for

But something may turn up
at any moment
and you have to be on your toes
waiting for it to happen

Out of the shadows of rented rooms
out of empty boxes   out of that thin space
between the mirror and the wall
and at the dead ends of streets hurrying by
when you do not intend to look
too closely   something

presents itself   and passes

I have a question

Listen

Waiting for your girl
at the airport   a stranger
rushes forward to meet you
He is mistaken of course
You look a little like his brother
It was the dark glasses and the hat
Perhaps he has some message
Perhaps you are his brother

We can't hear in the back row

Let me begin over   This is the way
it goes

A stranger rushes forward
at the airport
He pulls a revolver from his coat
and fires rapidly three shots
into your chest
He has mistaken you for an enemy
a blackmailer
a revolutionary coming to power
or his wife's lover

Lying there in all that confusion
who are you to say he was wrong

This is ridiculous

I pull the gun from my briefcase.
I say: Quick! Tell me everything you know.

VOICES ANSWERING BACK:
THE VAMPIRES

Rising in lamplight dying at dawn
grim burials in sheds and cellars
the rats scuttling through holes
and the days following in their tracks
exiled here we named the hours
since you first forgot to be afraid
once departed we became
only ourselves
with the salt on our tongues
and the cold for company
so deft in escape so practiced in dying
you might have learned from us
but each time the easiest trick worked
the brandished cross the empty mirror
you could not see us our steps upon the stairs
and while you stumbled after bats in the garden
we climbed quietly
from the upstairs window down the drainpipe
and through all the parties
you never heard what we were saying
it was something about desire
what we had in common even then
in your silence you feared us

always winning at the end but do you think
nothing lingered past dawn
shadowed among the gathered elms
do not be mistaken
we heard you walking through our dreams
we felt death moving between your hands
now we are waking early
practicing with sunlight
now we pass unharmed beneath your terrible star
eyes covered hands in our pockets
for the rules have always said
if you stop believing in us
we inherit everything

FIGURE WITH HYPODERMIC SYRINGE

from a painting by Francis Bacon

The man at the door has something to sell.
The prowling cars have someone to find.
Room's closing in, nothing left to take.
It's all the same, go in, go out, get on.

— I had a friend once but he died.

After a while even bleeding
begins to soften and goes away.
The man at the door is promising nothing.
I only sell the stuff; you take it from there.

— I had a woman once but she left.

The face on the wall is no face at all.
Any moment the real thing may arrive.
We do what we can with what we have at hand.
Who can say where it all begins.

— If I wasn't here I'd be somewhere else.

The window goes in, the window goes out.
The striped cloth creeps across the bed.
Cracks open in the wall. Needle's
in the arm, knocking's on the door.

— If only the hurt would keep the pain away.

SPLEEN

after Baudelaire

I am like the king of a rainy country,
rich yet idle, older than any passage
of years, scorning advice, bored
with his dogs, with the sports, the games,
even the bright falcon falling on the lawn.
Nor will his eyes ever turn beyond the balcony
where, upon the smooth stones of the courtyard,
his people are dying. No foolish song,
no fond clown's capering cheer him.
All the hard lines of waste he wears.
All the charmed beds grow damp and stale,
and his women, for whom every prince
seems beautiful, slipping from their clothes
in the softest of times, cannot
tease one smile from that thin face.
The scholar who makes his gold never found
charms to clear a body's dark element.
Nor, at the end, will steaming Roman baths,
remembered by the mighty to their last days,
warm this dying king. In his veins
a brackish water crawls, and in his eyes
only what has been forgotten lives.

THE LAST KING

Fragments from a Story

I. His Quest

There seemed no particular
purpose to it
the ambiguous landscapes
banal cliffs banal trees
thin   brittle as reeds
fringed with mists and.hard
to hold on   sometimes one way
sometimes the other way around

and monsters   huge but tired
as if they had seen too much
of this sort of thing
falling before the sword
pretending dead

and maidens   much less
beautiful than I expected
always asking to be taken
home after the battle

There seemed no way to discover
when it should be over
In their caves the wise men nodded
when I asked for directions

At the end I could count for myself
no bright thing to set upon a lady's hand
or riddle to charm a magician's ear
or potion to cheer my father's eyes

I found nothing very far from its surface
The blood crept close beneath the skin
and there was nowhere to go but home

bearing the names I brought with me
that inheritance I could
not help but carry

2. HE BECOMES KING AND BEGINS TO GROW OLD

The pale sun reverses my dream
but when I wake
here is the same day again
edged an hour closer to winter

When I turn the ancient face is upon the wall
and I have no words to answer

Why has the Queen kept to her chamber
Why have the unicorns abandoned our woods
Why has my son stayed
so long on his journey

How am I to present myself
when he arrives

My eyes have come to conceal nothing
My hands have returned to themselves
What can be done with them
I feel all that I could have changed

running through me like
sand in a glass

3. The Music, The Magician, and The Angel

At the appointed hour the clowns scatter
through our room their thin secrets
slippers   bells   bright hoods
but we are not amused

Again I am told
The clear music we loved
has departed forever from our age
But I sense a difficult disguise

Truly my magician says
the sharp light of it would blind us now
But I feel only wind on the walls
a disturbance of trees and perhaps
a different order

Remember I tell him I have paid my debts
offerings each morning
at the turning of the stairs
The angel has not appeared
and we have learned to live
with this disappointment

All difference is definition he replies
and the distance is the width of one hand
The angel has always been there
but it is not jasmine she desires

4. He Dreams of His Son, Who Will Not Return

We meet in a field at evening in springtime

For years I have been here
watching the road   for years
ordering the house for this return

But it is something different it is
a child's coat on his shoulders
and questions I cannot think to answer

It is my son who has wandered from shelter
an hour in the afternoon
pretending to have been away for years

The sun moves our shadows together
across the stones where we wait
He holds a bird in his coat

The touch of his hand loosens from me
everything I had taken to love
for years   for absence

But this is not the hour I wanted this is
changed   thé bird in his arms
We know it will not live for long

5. THE BATTLE

They stood where they were
until the wind cut them down

No one came to unstrap the shields
Relentlessly the rain
fell upon their open faces
No one came to close the eyes

Nor until snow found them
were their graves made

on the field where they
had spent all their lives

6. He Waits for His Death in a Field

Dawn gathered itself together while I
waited for snow to keep me warm
Where I lay the stiff grass broke
from my sides like spears
Kneeling down she found me
covered my eyes with her palms
and breathed all the cold from me
whispering in my ears
every promise we had
never made nor kept
until it did not matter

IN THE STORY OF THE SAME NAME

In the story of the same name
the end is always changing

Sometimes the children are saved
Sometimes they are devoured sometimes
they are falling and falling
until their eyes open

Often I go back to the beginning
or go around the long way
like a man looking for a cure
or a secret root or a road home

The years gather around the edges
wrinkling into dark
thinning into the shape of words
into the history in my hands
that changes when I look away

at the child falling past me
past the end of the story
where I cannot go to save him

THE ALCHEMIST

The long darkness of forks and spoons
possesses the table   a confusion of shadows
countless numbers folding and unfolding
at any time

begins with separations   divisions
rescued corners polished
to the edge of their elements

begins with the traced map
its smudged circles indicating
the many positions

of the keys   the glass eye and frosted jar
of the bandage   and the old mask

that each name be shaved first
of every sense save what it bears up
to carry by itself

like the stone   the prints before the door
going and coming
the coupling of voices passed over water
to where you happen to be as
if you meant
to be waiting

for such an arrangement
as the one glove remaindered from winter
could be assigned a shelf

begins with the tools which are provided

awl   hammer   saw
flask   glass   jackknife

and box   to carry the weight
and gauge what might be saved

wherein each instrument pretends
to observe a singular use

and so keep its place in the tabernacle

THREE APPLES ON A TABLE

Just as the day was going
Giacometti saw the space opening
between her eyes

not large enough to pass through
but a place to begin

When the light returned of course
it was gone

Her eyes fell back into a darkness
which left nothing behind

     It's gone he said

All around him thin unfinished men paused
their lacerated bones
arranged into whatever gestures
he could bear to see

The forest of faces murmured among themselves
Absence fell between the hands of others
like the skin of something you could touch

and distance always like a dream of itself

> *The whole thing hangs by a thread*
> *and you're always in danger*

Three apples lay on the sideboard
a coat on a chair

and a small figure continued walking
in a box between two boxes
which are houses

TO LORCA

Green, how much I want you green.
Green wind. Green branches.
The ship upon the sea
and the horse in the mountain.

Now the graves run all the way to the sea.
At this time of the year's turning even flowers
break. All the dying broods out of the land,
sits on top of boxes, forgets things,
and does not dream. Thirty times back
round your green sun, it was July that day
they came knocking. I do not know the hour, whether
the sky held sun, moon, or rain. But they left
the grave unmarked. *Do you see the wound*
I have from my breast to my throat? I see your face.
It is not easy to forget that face. All over a year
snow is descending, east and west hurrying down
like a storm of silence. I do not know your season,
yet that room you keep now must be cold, with no
quiet fire, and no book, with all those priests
gliding over you and not knowing, their ears
full of flowers. No one, not even you,
could hear them moving. *But I am no more I,*
nor is my house now my house. There are graves built
up to the moon on the mountain. They are full of bones
like snow, and no words. At the land's end cold water
climbs up the shore, and wants a bed, and slips back.
Green, how much I want you green. Here in March
I wait, soon to leave open the windows,

that green might flower up and the birds
wonder and laugh. Lorca, did they know
it was you they shot? *Green flesh, hair of green.*
The wind tears its eyes, and the snow
dries down into occupied ground. *Friend,
I come bleeding.* Your words are the seeds we
need still, though I imagine your face tells us
something we must forget to live.

THE ASYLUM YEARS

a poem for Christopher Smart

Madness frequently discovers itself
by unabandoned praise. Sane, could we
believe so much good of the world?
Poor Kit Smart, that harmless alcoholic,
he never loved clean linen.

Friends recalled that many times
he "shewed the disturbance of his mind
by falling upon his knees and saying
his prayers in the street." Surely

I too would have been embarrassed,
and gone out of my way to avoid him,
assuming no one might safely be that grateful.
Best, he thought, was praying naked in the rain.

They removed him to a quiet place
where he dug in the garden
like Adam, reciting to himself
the sayings of flowers.

For us, hopelessly sane, madness
seems a marvelous catastrophe.
But I suppose I never could have
liked the man, being shy of prayer,

and feel much safer years away
with his book, the defective light
of prisoned scribblings.
At the end he had only a cat to love.

Christopher, I will not be
too familiar with your name,
pray for me anyway on a street or in the rain,
that I may bless all I have at hand
and later learn to praise
what I cannot understand.

MAGRITTE: THE SONG OF THE GLASS KEYS AND THE CAPE OF STORMS

There is no country
where you could not paint a street
and walk down it
or a door in a wall or a window
inside a window
to look out on the green horizon

The secrets of these places
are not concealed or explained

though single words have been inscribed
upon the surface of things
souvenirs of the hunters who turned
their faces into their hands
remembered by a stranger leaning over a stone bridge
beside a lion

Thus the covering of dreams unfolds
to show the lining and these keys—

a clock which is the wind
a valise which is a valise

No object is so fond of its name
that another cannot be found to live with it

The lives of saints and sleep
melt into each other

while the tuba is consumed with the Lord's fire

while solutions return to their questions without asking
and you arrange the relics of evening
on the table of this strict light

Through the door in the wall
through the window inside the window
through the silence

you carry the fact of the shoes
the fact of the wind and of the woman
the fact of the rain

Great clouds creep across the earth
and the storm falls into them like a song

THE DREAM OF ROUSSEAU

Does she only pretend to sleep
and what does the lion think
sniffing at her neck

and then what happened?

The moonlight continued to fall
on the silver river and on the silver hills
and across each color of the gypsy's dress
like the songs her lute
propped between pillow and jug
might remember

Inside another dream

Yadwigha gently sleeping
Heard the sounds of a pipe
Played by a sympathetic charmer

while the moon touches each leaf and
each extravagant flower
pretending to be the color of daylight
as gentle as the velvet on the couch
even the serpents listen and the two lions
look a little surprised
at the sudden peace

Sir: "I am answering your kind letter immediately
in order to explain to you
the reason why the sofa in question is included.
The woman sleeping on the sofa
dreams that she is transported into the forest,
hearing ·the music of the snake charmer's instrument.
This explains why the sofa is in the picture.
I thank you
for your kind appreciation."

Later you told a friend
the sofa was there because of
a need for its color

You might have said
that the leopard and the man
struggle because
they happen to be there

Because they are there they understand
each other
and share the same dream
which holds them together for all
of their lives

in the middle of a jungle no one
could journey to

among those huge blossoms
no one has ever named
beneath that red sun
rising or going down
in the center of all that we can see

But no one wakes up
to find a lion leaning down
with the moon in his eyes
or a dark charmer finishing his song

and no one dies

as long as this light continues
to fall from the surface of the sky
touching evenly the edge of each leaf and

everything holds
its breath forever

ABOUT FLOWERS

So slowly she moves among the flowers
they seem to stop dying a moment
spangled vase of tulips asters in a bowl
chrysanthemums bending to a touch
her dreams too are like this
high grass floating near the beach
violets knitted through a field
the slow tides at their labors
everything that is beautiful rises
to her hand her thoughts do not pause
upon the day when flowers fail
to drink the thin cupped water
and petal by petal begin
unburdening themselves until
only stem and center stand
in the heavy sun of their undoing
but now they do not die they are safe
from every small danger of frost
if she were here I would think
nothing changes no one was ever afraid

SUNDAY

Among low familiar fields
the stones have their names
Flowers crowd at their sides
small cups thin flags
the neat and hyphened years
and the wind makes its way
toward winter

I have lodged myself in a box
surly and sad
with no one to visit

The Lady has four to remember
Her people she says all passed away
and have their places
but the roses by the plaques
cannot care for themselves
What could anyone ask
beyond this remembrance

What is it to be blessed
when all gifts of warmth
cower in the face of carvings

Out of marble ruins
impenetrable the hours of afternoon
become her own
The reasonings of passage
and the rites of flowers
may falter between her hands
but what remains rises
above the slow sway of fields
and blooms like bells
upon a danger of snow

I have hidden myself in a tree
where the wind bends down
and the bark bleeds secretly into my hands

Words I say
lie down a while in your white graves

WHERE YOU WERE

Here
I am unbuilding my house again
asking what should be saved
An old scrap of sky
lodged for a full year in that window
must be left behind

Wind from the river slips across the rug
Books fall from their shelves
as if to say
that just by moving   one space
it begins to be possible
to go

A wreckage of words
must be cleared from the floor
though any tenant would find these
as invisible as my departure
or yours

I number the boxes
remembering it is best to leave
nothing which could demand a return

to where you were   one touch from this
chair   this table   or that darkening window
now so far from me I find no
thing simple enough to serve
as a gift

I consider this page
but a poem is allowed to change only itself
to preserve merely what once was true
or not true

The way the wind touches your hair   here
as you turn   pause   or begin to smile
lovely in the last light
in the whispering of grass and the round
nodding of flowers   on an April hill
just as the dark comes down

WALKING ALONE

Where the wild poem is a substitute
For the woman one loves or ought to love,
One wild rhapsody a fake for another.

—*Wallace Stevens*

It is night. For hours I have been walking,
wanting to see you, hoping you might
appear suddenly by the side of the road,
on a bridge, or in the arc of headlights
bending toward me. I have continued

beyond any place you might conceivably be.
Sunk into a dark hollow, between trees
and stone, the river goes where it has to go.
In the cold air I construct long conversations:
whatever we wouldn't say if you were here.

I recite poems. I return home and write more.
You are, of course, attending within them,
beautiful and calm, near a window
or by a bridge before winter. I fix you
safely, where we might find each other.

But something comes between us, like glass
or water, a distance I cannot avoid.
We meet by accident and fall away.
I come back here, compose another poem,
and walk about at night reciting it to you.

Everything I conceive as possible returns
to an ordered page. I wish I were blind.
I wish my fingers would drop off.
What are they doing, writing all this again?

THE FORTUNE TELLER

Small troubles will cloud this month
If possible plan to stay near home
Be gracious   handle everything
with discretion   and use your charm
After the eighteenth things get better

                                        No

Then you will begin a long journey
You will meet a fair young woman
You will meet a tall dark gentleman
He will ask questions   Do not answer

                                        No

Traveling should be of a secret nature
Destinations must be considered temporary
What the stars sponsor they also take away
What I could tell you cannot be changed

                                        But

Shortly after leaving here
an old man will ask for money
Give him everything you have
Nevertheless on the way home your car

will strike a dog and
when you return he will be gone

                                        But
Why is your face in the glass so blurred
What you wish to know you carry with you
Even now all the world's time floats from us

Leave quickly   Do not listen further
you brought me   hands   face   fingers

Forgive me.   They are still yours.

THE ROOM AT THE END OF THE HALL

What can be carried with me
One bright edge with a thin stain

What has brought me this far
What sort of journey have I
tricked from the hedges what kind
of beast has followed me
into the first falling of snow
covering his path as he goes

I come upon myself
kneeling down at evening
before a landscape I do not remember

Some dark thing
swerves through the shorn fields
It is lost it is by itself

But here are my instruments
spread out upon the table
They beckon   they shine   I am

well prepared for the first incision

THE BURNING

The house is consumed but fire
does not touch you
The rush of flame leaves no scar
because you do not remember
why it should begin
to hurt

The blasted tree tightens to the rock
Rain drifts over grass
into another morning
Wrapped in the damp sheets of the journey
your life falls back into your hands
for a time

A looseness lifts from you
like ashes
but this is not the rescue

The roots deepen their risk
and the dark wound blossoms in the same corner
Hunters approach from the burning
beggars with baskets of words to sell
for bread

Embers scatter on the stones
and the sea carries them away

The moon swings the tide toward home
At bottom there is nothing to touch

while your nails grow a little and your hair
inches to the edge of the polished cover

EIGHT LANDSCAPES FROM THE
TAROT DECK

The fear began at the borders of fire
and not in the darkness

In the late haze of sun trees
moved against their circles

and into the whisperings
from the middle air

Not everything works

The river remains   the light shifts

We are standing in the yard of a used-up school
in an August afternoon
heavy with the hidden sound of
flies trapped between the wire and the window
following us
when we move

The things we touch
bear us up and change with us

There may be no message

but nothing survives us
without a name

given away   altered   and given back

part of the long history of strangers

become
figures framed upon the pattern of your sleep
the plague of your dreams
and a thread of safety
between both

The turn of the deck leads to an edge
where the high air shakes

On the water the circles widen

Reversed
they gather one
into another toward the center
Either way the surface
restores itself

When the cards reply you say they are

returning
to us

The hanged man inverted shows him on his feet

Remember how the edge of the sky
when it touched your hand
drew that thin scar

Under the moon and the dew falling
a marked path loses itself in the horizon
A crayfish   emblematic of Cancer
ruled over by the Moon   crawls through thick water
toward land   suggesting

twilight   deception   and error

The figures of coming and going
appear in 78 changes

By one account the cards contain
all knowledge of the universe collected
by ancient Egyptians
who agreed to transmit this knowledge
covering tablets with symbols
thus concealing
the doctrine

The buzzing of what is kept from us
becomes part of the stillness of the afternoon

The parched walls bear it out
and the wind picks it up for itself

cracked stones
blistered paint and a hoop over the door
rusted grass in the yard

growing back

into a place to end as good
as any

THE END OF THE STORY
OF THE WHITE BIRD

for Edward Gorey

Then, as it should have been Morning,

no one could doubt
that what the bird had said was true.

You will have no help from me,
replied the mirror, clouding over.
His lordship waded into the stream
and was swept away.

The Queen, nevertheless, was pleased.
And why not, said Jack.
The Good Son descended from the tower,
saddled his horse and rode off.

And the witch never found the boy, or the money.
Opening the bag, a dog jumped out and killed her.
Meanwhile, fire destroyed the castle, crying—
Finished, finished, finished!

And one Echo answered— Oh,
where are my pretty stones?
Pieces of gold fell heavily through the water,
and the dark flood swayed,

while the princess, again lost
in the maze, continued to ask—
But what was I supposed to remember?
Hearing her voice, the statues wept.

And the white bird climbed
up the ladder of the wind, into the sun.

MERLIN

The grass rose like a dream around him

The names divided in the story he had chosen

    Some are disguises
    Others the beginnings of themselves
    Only a few go all the way

Another story began   he grew younger

    When they move into each other
    you cannot be sure
    where you are or what
    is supposed to happen next

The pale stars tilted above him like a chart

    Only what is remembered is real

Something like singing met him by the water
in the shape of no song he could remember

When you hear one it is yours

The story divided   another began
clear and full of silence

an open window   a cave
of wind   the long grass
between the forest and those fields

like a dream of sleep inside a dream

Like the shape of dark water
unraveling into the earth

the song covered him with the words that it knew

ICE

I

The wind falls back across the snow

Silence leans in the doorway
just as pale as you had imagined

Why invite him further

That song is a simple one
easy to learn hard to forget

You know how it goes
You remember

2

At night the cold
sinks its teeth in your cheek
In the morning the cold
leaves its ghost in your breath

You discover what continues to live
inside the splinters of things
hiding   pretending to be a secret

inside the stones full of tiny flames
inside the smoke floating above the trees
inside the ice that looks back
into nothing but itself

3

Each day the snow falls
repeating and repeating its one line

You ask for news and you get
another list

and the end of winter arrives
with the names of the missing
and the same question

Who do you know
this time

At the edge of light
the wolves take up their howling

They have always been there
inside their hunger

4
I give you what I can
a coat and a compass
matches in a tin box

I give you
this shelter

Step into it
and silence touches you
everywhere

When you speak
your words drop to the floor
When you break them open
there are more words inside

mirror   knife   ice
fire   smoke   stone

You know how it goes
You remember

the song of wind in the branch
the message of light across the snow
the sign of your breath

frozen into stars on the clear glass

THE PALACE AT 4 A.M.

Once the sculpture is made, I have a tendency to rediscover in it, transformed and displaced, images, impressions, facts which have profoundly moved me (often without my knowing it), forms which I feel are very close to me, although I am often incapable of identifying them, which always makes them more disturbing . . .

—*Alberto Giacometti*

I

Sometimes it will be necessary
to discard everything

when the space widens between your eye and hers

and simply turn
away
or move further back

when darkness crowds about her face
and flowers grow unmanageable

A few fragments may be trusted
In the midst of danger
a small opening presents itself

Inside the palace it is
four o'clock in the morning

The bones of a great bird hang
as if flying
near the roofless tower

The image of a woman stands in front of three curtains

2

The rain begins suddenly
falling between the faces
of people hurrying out of the way

Just by trying to see clearly
the difficulty arrives and then
there is no end to it

Once is enough

A blind man stretches out his hand

Rain spills across the street
over painted chairs in front of the café
which closed hours ago

You make a single mark and the light
rushes past you to prove another mistake

Nothing will stand still

Across from the woman   beneath the bird
the bleached spine of an animal
dangles in its cage

3

You could say the man in the rain
walks in a straight line down the street
as if he knew where to go

You could imagine him searching
or leaving someone behind
or merely anxious
to return home

You could say the bird in the palace is waiting
though it does not wait   it just
remains
pieces of bone on a string

Nor does the tall figure
point toward anything in particular but only
whatever lies at the end of his arm
wherever he is placed

in a room   or a garden   beside a wall

he indicates
any direction

It is useless to expect a sign
unless the sign

has always been there

4

When a clay man raised his arms
and opened his hands this
soon became unbearable

Perhaps he was trying
to reveal something which you knew
could not be there

Sometimes it is necessary
to remove everything but the bone

to search beneath the skin
for the skull
the dark pockets beneath the eyes
just to be able to see

that girl sitting at the other end of the room

To discover where he is going
the blind man stretches out his fingers

a chair   a wall   a window

Just by looking   each day
everything changes   the retreat begins
gathering it into the walls

and such deceptions as these
become necessary

souvenirs touched by the knife

no more than dust pasted together into an arm
or a forest of faces

a matchbox of heads
a palace of sticks and glass